First World War
and Army of Occupation
War Diary
France, Belgium and Germany

42 DIVISION
Divisional Troops
Divisional Ammunition Column
19 March 1917 - 29 March 1919

WO95/2649/3

The Naval & Military Press Ltd
www.nmarchive.com
Published in association with The National Archives

Published by

The Naval & Military Press Ltd

Unit 10 Ridgewood Industrial Park,

Uckfield, East Sussex,

TN22 5QE England

Tel: +44 (0) 1825 749494

www.naval-military-press.com

www.nmarchive.com

This diary has been reprinted in facsimile from the original. Any imperfections are inevitably reproduced and the quality may fall short of modern type and cartographic standards.

© **Crown Copyright**
Images reproduced by permission of The National Archives, London, England, 2015.

Contents

Document type	Place/Title	Date From	Date To
Heading	WO95/2649/3		
Heading	42nd Divl Ammn Column Mar 1917-Mar 1919.		
Heading	War Diary Of 42nd Divisional Ammunition Column. From March 19th 1917. To March 31st 1917. (Volume III)		
Heading	Secret		
Miscellaneous	Officer i/c R.A. Reeds G.H.L.		
War Diary	Drucat. Reference Abbeville 14 France 1/100,0000 K.5	19/03/1917	30/03/1917
Heading	War Diary Of 42nd Divisional Ammunition Column From April 1st 1917 To April 30th 1917 (Volume IV)		
Heading	Secret		
War Diary	Drucat Ref Abbeville 14 France 1/100,000 K.5	03/04/1917	03/04/1917
War Diary	Saint Sauveur (Ref Amiens 17 France 1/100,000 C.I.)	04/04/1917	04/04/1917
War Diary	Hamelet Ref Amiens 17 France 1/1000000 C.I.	05/04/1917	05/04/1917
War Diary	Froissy (Ref Amiens 17 France 1/100,000 I2	06/04/1917	29/04/1917
Heading	War Diary Of 42nd Divisional Ammunition Column From May 1st 1917 To May 31st 1917 (Volume V)		
War Diary	Le Mesnil Bruntel	02/05/1917	02/05/1917
War Diary	Villers Faucon	03/05/1917	25/05/1917
War Diary	Bus	31/05/1917	31/05/1917
Heading	War Diary Of 42nd Divisional Ammunition Column. From 1-6-17 To 30-6-17 Volume 3		
War Diary	Bus	30/04/1917	30/06/1917
Heading	War Diary Of 42nd Divisional Ammunition Column From 1.7.17 To 31.7.17.		
War Diary	Bus.	10/07/1917	31/07/1917
Heading	War Diary Of 42nd D.A.C. From 1-8-17 To 31-8-17 Vol. VI		
War Diary	Poperinghe	31/08/1917	31/08/1917
War Diary	Bus	01/08/1917	15/08/1917
War Diary	Achiet-Le-Petit	21/08/1917	21/08/1917
War Diary	Godewaersvelde	23/08/1917	23/08/1917
War Diary	Bus	25/08/1917	26/08/1917
War Diary	Godewaersvelde	26/08/1917	26/08/1917
War Diary	Proven	26/08/1917	27/08/1917
War Diary	Watou	29/08/1917	31/08/1917
Heading	War Diary Of 42nd D.A.C. From 1-9-17 To 30-9-17. Vol VII		
War Diary	Poperinghe	01/09/1917	30/09/1917
Heading	War Diary Of 42nd D.A.C. From Oct 1st 1917 To Oct 31st 1917.		
War Diary	Wormhoudt	01/10/1917	01/10/1917
War Diary	Teteghem	02/10/1917	02/10/1917
War Diary	Coxyde	03/10/1917	14/10/1917
War Diary	Furnes	16/10/1917	24/10/1917
War Diary	Kerke Panne	31/10/1917	31/10/1917
Heading	War Diary Of 42nd Div. Ammn Col From 1-11-17 To 30-11-17 Vol VIII		
War Diary	Kerke Panne	01/11/1917	21/11/1917
War Diary	Ghyvelde	23/11/1917	23/11/1917

War Diary	Wormhoudt	24/11/1917	24/11/1917
War Diary	Zermezeele	25/11/1917	25/11/1917
War Diary	St Marie Cappel	26/11/1917	26/11/1917
War Diary	Quernes	29/11/1917	30/11/1917
Heading	War Diary Of 42nd Div Amm Column.		
War Diary	Robecq.	01/12/1917	01/12/1917
War Diary	Bethune	01/12/1917	16/12/1917
Heading	War Diary Of 42nd Div. Amm. Column From 1st Jan. 1918 To 1st Feb. 1918. Volume. XIII		
War Diary	Bethune	01/01/1918	31/01/1918
Heading	War Diary Of 42nd Div. Column From 1-2-18 To 28-2-18. Volumn XIII		
War Diary	Bethune	01/02/1918	16/02/1918
Heading	42nd Divisional Ammunition Column R.F.A. March 1918		
Heading	War Diary Of 42nd Div Amm Column From 1/3/18. To 31/3/18 Vol. XV		
War Diary	Gonnehem	01/03/1918	23/03/1918
War Diary	Gauchen Legal	24/03/1918	24/03/1918
War Diary	Bienvillers Au Bois	25/03/1918	25/03/1918
War Diary	Ayette	26/03/1918	26/03/1918
War Diary	Essarts	26/03/1918	26/03/1918
War Diary	Bienvillers Au Bois	27/03/1918	31/03/1918
Heading	42nd Divisional Ammunition Column. April 1918		
Heading	War Diary Of 42nd Div. Amm. Column. From 1st April 1918. To. 30th April 1918 Vol XVI		
War Diary	Gaudiempre	01/04/1918	01/04/1918
War Diary	Souastre	05/04/1918	18/04/1918
War Diary	Couin	23/04/1918	23/04/1918
Heading	War Diary Of 42nd Div. Ammn. Column From 1st May 1918 To 31st May 1918 Volume XVII		
War Diary	Couin	01/05/1918	27/05/1918
Heading	War Diary Of 42nd Div. Amm. Column. From 1/6/18 To 30-6-18Vol. XVIII		
War Diary	Couin	01/06/1918	23/06/1918
Heading	War Diary Of 42nd Div. Amm. Column From 1/7/18. To. 31/7/18 Vol. XIX		
War Diary	Couin.	01/07/1918	05/07/1918
War Diary	Louvencourt	16/07/1918	24/07/1918
Heading	War Diary Of 42nd Div. Ammunition Column R.F.A. From 1st August To 31st August 1918. Volume XX		
War Diary	Louvencourt	01/08/1918	24/08/1918
War Diary	Bertrancourt	25/08/1918	25/08/1918
War Diary	Bucquoy	26/08/1918	26/08/1918
War Diary	Miraumont	29/08/1918	30/08/1918
Heading	42nd Div. Ammunition Column. War Diary. Vol XXI September 1918		
War Diary	Grevillers	01/09/1918	03/09/1918
War Diary	Thilloy	04/09/1918	04/09/1918
War Diary	Barastre	07/09/1918	08/09/1918
War Diary	Miraumont	09/09/1918	09/09/1918
War Diary	Barastre	22/09/1918	25/09/1918
War Diary	Bertincourt	27/09/1918	27/09/1918
Heading	War Diary Of 42nd Divisional Ammunition Column. From 1st October 1918. To 31st October 1918. Volume. XXII		

War Diary	Bertincourt.	01/10/1918	01/10/1918
War Diary	Trescault	02/10/1918	10/10/1918
War Diary	Esnes	11/10/1918	11/10/1918
War Diary	Beauvois	12/10/1918	15/10/1918
War Diary	Jeune Bois	15/10/1918	21/10/1918
War Diary	Prayelle	23/10/1918	24/10/1918
War Diary	Solesmes	24/10/1918	27/10/1918
Heading	War Diary Of 42nd Divisional Ammunition Column. From 1st November 1918. To 30th November 1918. Volume XXIII.		
War Diary	Romeries	01/11/1918	06/11/1918
War Diary	Pont Billon	07/11/1918	07/11/1918
War Diary	Herbignies	12/11/1918	12/11/1918
War Diary	La Corne	19/11/1918	29/11/1918
Heading	War Diary Of 42nd Division Amm. Column. From 1-12-1918 To 31-12-1918. Volume XXIV		
War Diary	La Corne	01/12/1918	01/12/1918
War Diary	La Corne	14/12/1918	14/12/1918
War Diary	Marpent	15/12/1918	15/12/1918
War Diary	Lobbes	18/12/1918	18/12/1918
Heading	War Diary Of 42nd Divisional Ammunition Column. From:- 1st January 1919. To:- 31st January 1919 Volume XXV.		
War Diary	Chatelineau	01/01/1919	01/01/1919
War Diary	Belgium	31/01/1919	31/01/1919
Heading	War Diary Of 42nd Div. Amm. Column (incld 42nd T.M.B.) From 1st Feby 1919. To 28th Feby 1919. Volume XXVI		
War Diary	Chatelineau	01/02/1919	01/02/1919
War Diary	Belgium	28/02/1919	28/02/1919
Heading	War Diary Of 42nd Div. Amm. Column & T.M.B. From. 1.3.1919. To 31st 3.1919. Volume XXVII		
War Diary	Chatelineau	01/03/1919	01/03/1919
War Diary	Belgium	14/03/1919	29/03/1919

WO 95
2649/3

42ND DIVISION

42ND DIVL AMMN COLUMN
MAR 1917-MAR 1919

Vol 2

CONFIDENTIAL.

War Diary

of

42ND Divisional Ammunition Column.

(Volume III.)

from March 19th 1917. to March 31st 1917.

SECRET

M 195

Officer i/c
R.A. Records
G.H.Q.

Herewith please copy
of WAR DIARY for the month
of MARCH – 1917 forwarded
for favour of retention.

[signature]
Major
Comdg 42nd D.A.C

31/3/17

Army Form C. 2118.

WAR DIARY
or
INTELLIGENCE SUMMARY

(Erase heading not required.)

42ND DIVISIONAL AMMUNITION COLUMN

Instructions regarding War Diaries and Intelligence Summaries are contained in F. S. Regs., Part II. and the Staff Manual respectively. Title Pages will be prepared in manuscript.

Place	Date	Hour	Summary of Events and Information	Remarks and references to Appendices
DRUCAT. Reference ABBEVILLE .14 FRANCE 1/100,000 K.5	19.3.17.		42nd D.A.C. came into being. Headquarters, No1 Section, No3 Section arrived at DRUCAT. (ABBEVILLE.14 FRANCE 1/100,000 K.5) No 2 Section arrived at LE PRESSEIL (ABBEVILLE.14 FRANCE 1/100,000 K.5). No1 Section comprised of late 210 B.A.C. and commanded by Lt NUTTALL.F No 2 Section " " 211 B.A.C " " CAPT. HIGHTON. L No 3 Section " " 212 B.A.C. " " CAPT. SOWLER F. Headquarters not yet formed.	
	20.3.17.		Capt-SOWLER F. No 3 Section assumes temporary command. 2/Lt FINCH.H } No1 Section attached B.2.I.O. 1.O.R } 2/Lt HARTLEY.R. No1 Section 2 q.O.R. from No1 Section } proceeded BOIS DU L'ABBÉE (ABBEVILLE.14 FRANCE 1/100,000 K.5) on detached duty 2 q.O.R. " " No 2 Section }	↑ ↑
	21.3.17.		1. O.R. posted from No1 Section to B.2.I.O. 1. O.R. posted from B.2.I.O to No1 Section.	
	22.3.17.		MAJOR DOBSON. B.P. posted to command 42nd D.A.C. from 210 Brigade. R.F.A. CAPT HIGHAM.T.A. " " No1 Section " late 212 Brigade R.F.A Lt. NUTTALL.F posted as adjutant from No1 Section. (R.A.D. 928 d/22.3.17) 2. O.R posted to Headquarters from C.21.D 1. O.R admitted to hospital.	

2449 Wt. W14957/M90 750,000 1/16 J.B.C. & A. No. 3 P. Forms/C.2118/12.

WAR DIARY or INTELLIGENCE SUMMARY

(Erase heading not required.)

Army Form C. 2118

Place	Date	Hour	Summary of Events and Information	Remarks and references to Appendices
	22.3.17		Capt SOWLER F. No 3 Section } proceeded to Bois de L'ABBEY (Reference ABBEVILLE 14 FRANCE 1/100,000 ave K.5) on detached duty 2. O.R. from " " " }	
	23.3.17		1. O.R (No 3 Section) rejoined from furlough to U.K. 1. O.R (No 2 Section) admitted to hospital	
	24.3.17		LT SCOWCROFT C.I } posted from No 2 Section to D.2.11 2. O.R. LT BUCK L.} } posted to No 2 Section from D 2.11 2. O.R. }	R.A.O. 938. d/23.3.17.
			2. O.R. posted from A 2.10 to No 1 Section 2. O.R. " No 1 Section to A 2.10 2/LT WALMSLEY. T.H. No 1 Section proceeded on leave to U.K.	
	25.3.17		9. O.R. posted from No 1 Section to headquarters 7. O.R. " " No 2 " " " 6. O.R. " " No 3 " " " Divisional Trench Mortar Batteries attached as supernumeraries Above consists of 7 officers. 133 O.R. 12 2" mortars.	
	26.3.17		254 O.R posted from RH & RFA report to this unit to complete establishment Above draft posted as follows :- HdQrs 2. O.R. No 1 Section 72.O.R. No 2 Section 64 O.R. No 3 Section 116 draft inspected by B.G.R.A.	
	27.3.17		4. O.R. (No 2 Section) attached headquarters 210 Bde R.F.A.	
	28.3.17		2/LT BEARD No 3 Section 30 O.R proceeded on French Mortar Course at VAUX EN AMIENOIS (Reference AMIENS 1Y FRANCE 1/50,000 C.1)	

Army Form C. 2118

WAR DIARY
or
INTELLIGENCE SUMMARY
(Erase heading not required.)

Instructions regarding War Diaries and Intelligence Summaries are contained in F. S. Regs., Part II. and the Staff Manual respectively. Title Pages will be prepared in manuscript.

Place	Date	Hour	Summary of Events and Information	Remarks and references to Appendices
	28·3·19 (continued)		Capt HIGHTON & } No 2 Section Temporarily attached to hospital 2. O.R. 2. O.R. from No 1 Section admitted to hospital. The following drawn to complete establishment from Advance Horse Transport Depot ABBEVILLE (Reference ABBEVILLE 1A FRANCE 1/100,000 K.5.) for Headquarters 7 vehicles 24 animals. for No 1 Section 23 Vehicles 110 animals	
	29.3.19.		6 O.R. proceeded on leave to U.K.	
	30.3.19.		The following drawn to complete establishment from Advance Horse Transport Depot ABBEVILLE (Reference ABBEVILLE 1A. FRANCE 1/100,000 K.5.) for No 2 Section 11 G.S. wagons 66 animals. 8 limbered G.S. 16 animals. for No 3 Section 14 G.S. wagons 64 animals. 1 water cart 2 animals. Also 100 horses with harness. These latter were divided amongst the 3 Section to complete establishment. The whole of this month since the formation of this unit has been spent in organising the various units, requisitioning horses, vehicles & general equipment. This reorganisation & equipment is almost complete. The health of the units has been good. J.B.C. & A. A.D.S.S./Forms/C. 2118.	

Vol 3

CONFIDENTIAL

WAR DIARY

of

42ND DIVISIONAL AMMUNITION COLUMN

from APRIL 1st 1917 to APRIL 30th 1917

(VOLUME IV)

= SECRET =

Army Form C. 2118.

WAR DIARY
INTELLIGENCE SUMMARY.
(Erase heading not required.)

Instructions regarding War Diaries and Intelligence Summaries are contained in F. S. Regs., Part II. and the Staff Manual respectively. Title pages will be prepared in manuscript.

I

Place	Date	Hour	Summary of Events and Information	Remarks and references to Appendices
DRUCAT (Ref ABBEVILLE 14 FRANCE 1/100,000 K.5)	April 1st		D.A.C. inspected by B.G.R.A.	
	3.4.19		7 O.R. proceeded on 10 days leave to U.K.	
			1 O.R. posted to this unit from R.H. & R.F.A. Base.	
			254 horses drawn complete with harness from Advanced Horse Transport Depot ABBEVILLE (Ref ABBEVILLE 14, FRANCE 1/100,000 K.5.)	O.K.
			43 horses drawn from REMOUNTS. ABBEVILLE (Ref ABBEVILLE 14 FRANCE 1/100,000 K.5.)	
			The equipment of this unit by this date is complete except in the case of minor articles.	
SAINT SAUVEUR (Ref AMIENS 19 FRANCE 1/100,000 C.1.)	4.4.19.		Proceeded from DRUCAT (Ref ABBEVILLE 14 FRANCE 1/100,000 K.5) to SAINT SAUVEUR (Ref AMIENS 19 FRANCE 1/100,000 C.1.)	
			No 1 Section proceeded to ARGOEUVES (Ref AMIENS 19 FRANCE 1/100,000 C.1.)	
			Headquarters & the sections billeted at the above places respectively.	
			1 O.R. to hospital	
HAMELET (Ref AMIENS 19 FRANCE 1/100,000 C.1.)	5.4.19		Proceeded by march route to HAMELET (Ref AMIENS 19 FRANCE 1/100,000 G.2.)	O.S./
			Billeted for the night at the above place.	
			CAPT. BOWLER. F. } rejoined from BOIS L'ABBEE (Ref ABBEVILLE 14 FRANCE 1/100,000 K.5.)	
			2/LT HARTLEY. R. No 1 Section	
			5 O.R.	
FROISSY (Ref AMIENS 19 FRANCE 1/100,000 I.2)	6.4.19		100 horses	
			Proceeded by march route to FROISSY (Ref AMIENS 19. I.2).	O.S.J
			This unit was split up for the move from DRUCAT (Ref ABBEVILLE 14. FRANCE 1/100,000 K.5.), No1 Section and a portion of No3 Section being attached to 210 Brigade R.F.A.; No2 Section + a portion of No3 Section being attached to 211 Brigade R.F.A. The above sections provided the transport for the 210 Brigade R.F.A. and 211 Brigade R.F.A. respectively	

WAR DIARY
or
INTELLIGENCE SUMMARY.
(Erase heading not required.)

Army Form C. 2118.

II

Place	Date	Hour	Summary of Events and Information	Remarks and references to Appendices
FROISSY. (Ref AMIENS 1/4 FRANCE I 2) 1/40,000	7.4.17		2/Lt WALMSLEY. T.H rejoined from furlough to U.K.	
			CAPT CARUS. F.X.S } 210 Brigade R.F.A attached for duty. 1.O.R (F.X.S)	A.S.J.
			Capt CARUS. F.X.S assumes Temporary command of No 2 Section	
			18 hdrs 4.5 ammunition drawn up to establishment by No 1 & No 2 Sections	
			1. O.R (No 2 Section) to hospital.	
			2/Lt McKENZIE No 2 Section	
			2/Lt ENTWISLE No 3 Section } proceed to HAMEL (Ref FRANCE 62 c/40,000 J.18) for Temporary attachment to 46 D.A.C	
			80 O.R. from No 3 Section	
			150 horses from No 3 Section	
			Inspection of Lines by H.G.R.A 3rd Corps.	
	8.4.17		18. O.R. proceed on 10 days leave to U.K.	
			No 1 Section (Gun Section only) proceed to TEMIEUX LA FOSSE (Ref FRANCE 62 c/40,000 D 28) for Temporary attachment to 48th Division. The above gun section will supply ammunition to 211 Brigade	A.S.J.
			S.A.A. drawn up to establishment	
			2/Lt BUCK. L. proceeds on detached duty to C Corps Ammunition Park.	
			2/Lt BEARD. H.E No 3 Section } return from course of Instruction at VAUX EN AMIENOIS. (Ref AMIENS 1/4 France C.1.) 1/40,000	
			3. 1. O.R.	
	9.4.17		2. O.R (No 2 Section) to hospital.	A.S.J.
			Gas equipment fitted and issued.	

WAR DIARY
INTELLIGENCE SUMMARY
(Erase heading not required.)

Army Form C. 2118.

III

Instructions regarding War Diaries and Intelligence Summaries are contained in F.S. Regs., Part II. and the Staff Manual respectively. Title pages will be prepared in manuscript.

Place	Date	Hour	Summary of Events and Information	Remarks and references to Appendices
	9.4.17		LT RICHARDS D210 ⎫ Temporarily attached from 210 Brigade R.F.A.	
			LT BROOKE F. C210 ⎬	
			2/LT HARTLEY. GP B210 ⎭	
			6. O.R.	
	11.4.17		3. O.R. from No 1 Section ⎫ admitted to hospital	
			4. O.R. " " 3 " ⎭	
			2. O.R. attached 4th FIELD SURVEY Company R.E	
			6 O.R. rejoined from leave to U.K.	a.s.g
	13.4.17		Capt MARKS H.N rejoins unit & is posted to No 2 Section	
			LT SMITH E. D210 ⎫ Temporarily attached from 210 Brigade R.F.A.	
			1. O.R. ⎭	
			LT RICHARDS ⎫ rejoins 210 Brigade R.F.A.	
			1. O.R. ⎭	
			18. O.R. proceeded on 10 days leave to U.K.	
	14.4.17		1 O.R admitted to hospital	
	15.4.17		7 O.R rejoin from furlough to U.K.	
			12. O.R. posted to unit from R.H.& R.F.A. Depot.	
	17.4.17		8. O.R posted to unit from R.H.& R.F.A. Depot	
			No 2 Section proceed to LE MESNIL BRUNTEL (Reference FRANCE 62c⎯ 0.1M)	
			No 2 Section from this date are employed in carting for repair of roads in the area of IIIrd Corps.	
	18.4.17		5 O.R. proceed on furlough to U.K	

WAR DIARY or INTELLIGENCE SUMMARY

Army Form C. 2118.

Place	Date	Hour	Summary of Events and Information	Remarks and references to Appendices
18.4	18.4.17		1.O.R from No 1 Section } admitted to hospital. 1.O.R from No 2 Section }	
	19.4.17		Capt PHILP. C.H.G (R.A.M.C) attached for duty to unit	A.S.I.
	21.4.17		1.O.R from No 3 Section admitted to hospital. 2/LT RIVETT. C.E. No 3 Section admitted to hospital.	
			Capt CARUS F.X.S LT SMITH R. LT BROOK S.F. } rejoin 210 Brigade R.F.A 2/LT HARTLEY G.P 4 O.R.	
			2 Officers 80 O.R. } rejoin unit from temporary attachment to 46 D.A.C 150 horses	A.S.I.
			Capt MARKS. H.N. assumes command of No 2 Section.	
	22.4.17		Unit proceeds by march route to LE MESNIL BRUNTEL (Reference FRANCE 1/40,000 62c O.17)	A.S.I.
LE MESNIL BRUNTEL (FRANCE) 1/40,000 62c O.17	23.4.17		No 2 Section Gun section only proceed by march route to BOUCLY (reference FRANCE 1/40,000 62 S 24). This Gun Section from this date is attached to 59th Division along with 210 Brigade R.F.A. No 3 Section from this date takes over the work on the roads previously performed by No 2 Section. 1 O.R rejoin from furlough to U.K. 2/LT STUTTARD. T. attends Artillery Course of Instruction at VAUX EN AMIENOIS (Reference AMIENS 1Y C1.) FRANCE 1/100,000	

WAR DIARY or **INTELLIGENCE SUMMARY**
(Erase heading not required.)

Army Form C. 2118.

V

Place	Date	Hour	Summary of Events and Information	Remarks and references to Appendices
	24.4.17		1 O.R (No 1 Section) admitted to hospital.	
	25.4.17		LT HUGHES, J.E. RFA posted to this unit and temporarily attached to R.A Headquarters 42nd Division. (R.A.O. 5 d/25.4.17) from 21st unit	
			MAJOR DOBSON. B.P (OC 42nd D.A.C) appointed to command R A Troops at LE MESNIL BRUNTEL (Ref FRANCE 62C.O.17) 49000	
	27.4.17		2/Lt C.A E. JOLIFFE (R.F.A. T.F) (R.A.O. 5 d/25.4.17) attached to command 42nd D.A.C (Authority G.H Q letter No 346 B d/144.17)	A.S.J
			MAJOR. B.P DOBSON posted to command B 210. (R.A.O.13. d/27.4.17)	
	28.4.17		18 O.R proceed on 10 days furlough to U.K.	
			18 D.R return from leave to U.K.	
			Draft of 36 O.R posted to unit from R.H + R.F.A Depot.	
			Lieut J.E. HUGHES. appointed adjutant	
			Lieut E. NUTTALL posted to 210 Brigade	
			LT E. NUTTALL to act as adjutant during temporary attachment of LT HUGHES to R.A. Headquarters (R.A Memo 354 d/28.4.17)	A.S.J
	29.4.17		12 D.R posted from unit to 211 Brigade } (R.A Memo 38 d/29.4.17)	
			14 O.R posted " " " 210 Brigade }	

A.S. Jolliffe, 2/Lt.
Comdg. 42nd. D.A.C.
30/4/17.

Vol 4

CONFIDENTIAL.

WAR DIARY

of

42ND DIVISIONAL AMMUNITION COLUMN

FROM MAY 1st 1917 to MAY 31st 1917.

(VOLUME V)

42nd Divisional Ammunition Column. R.F.A.

WAR DIARY
or
INTELLIGENCE SUMMARY.
(Erase heading not required.)

Army Form C. 2118.

Place	Date	Hour	Summary of Events and Information	Remarks and references to Appendices
LE MESNIL BRUNTEL	2/5/17		Column proceeded by road to VILLERS FAUCON. Sheet 62c. E.22. L/ro No 3 Section to MARQUAIX Sheet 62c. K.14. - Route - LE CATELET - CARTIGNY - BOUCLY - ROISEL.	A.S.1
"	"		No I Section [attached [48 Div Arty]] rejoins unit.	
"	"		Relieved 48 D.A.C. [L/ro No I Section], took over A.R.P.	
"	"		No I Section 48 D.A.C. attached for supply of ammunition to B.C.n.II 240th Brigade.	
"	"		Disposition of Unit. Sheet 62c.:-	
"	"		Headquarters E 28 a 60.	
"	"		No I Sect " 22 c 8.1.	
"	"		" 2 " , 29 d 30.	
"	"		" 3 " K 8 d 25	
VILLERS FAUCON	3/5/17		Lieut. NUTTALL relinquishes duties as Adjutant and posted to 210th Brigade.	A.S.2
"	"		" HUGHES assumes duties as Adjutant	
"	8/5/17		2/Lt. FORTH posted to 211th Brigade R.F.A	A.S.2
"	"		" WALKER " " "	
"	"		" RIVETT rejoined from Hospital.	
"	9/5/17		" HAME posted " 59th Div: Arty.	A.S.2

Army Form C. 2118.

WAR DIARY
of
INTELLIGENCE SUMMARY.
(Erase heading not required.)

Instructions regarding War Diaries and Intelligence Summaries are contained in F.S. Regs. Part II. and the Staff Manual respectively. Title pages will be prepared in manuscript.

Place	Date	Hour	Summary of Events and Information	Remarks and references to Appendices
VILLERS FAUCON	10/5/17		The I Section 48 II.A.C. rejoins its Unit.	
"	19/5/17	Noon	S.A.A. and Grenades etc as A.R.P. handed over to 2nd Cavalry Division	a.s.1
"	21/5/17	"	Gun Ammunition " " " 59th Aus. Artillery	
"	22/5/17	"	Unit [Less 4 Horseys Wagons No. 1 Section] proceeded by route march to Bus. Sheet 57cT 024.	a.s.2
			Route LIERAMONT — NURLU — ETRICOURT
			4 Horsey Wagons of No. 1 Section attached 59th II.A.C. accompanying 298th Brigade R.F.A.
			Distribution of Unit Sheet 57c :—
			Headquarters O.24 c 58
			No. 1 Section O.24 b 15
			" 2 " O.24 c 98
			" 3 " O.27 d 87
	23/5/17		Gun Ammunition as A.R.P. NEUVILLE taken over from 20th II.A.C.	
	25/5/17		Unit relieves 20th II.A.C.	a.s.2

Army Form C. 2118.

WAR DIARY
or
INTELLIGENCE SUMMARY.
(Erase heading not required.)

Instructions regarding War Diaries and Intelligence Summaries are contained in F. S. Regs., Part II. and the Staff Manual respectively. Title pages will be prepared in manuscript.

Place	Date	Hour	Summary of Events and Information	Remarks and references to Appendices
Bus	31/1/17		18-180 Arms Wagons with Personnel Horses etc proceed to Clay Quarry Sheet 57c V.3.c.d. for attachment to 59th Divl Artillery.	AS/.
			The following arrivals and departures for the month were:—	
			Posted from R.H. & R.F.A. Base Depot. 115 other ranks.	
			" " 211th Brigade R.F.A 3 " "	
			" to 210th Brigade 39 " "	
			" " 211th " 70 " "	
			" " Base. R.H. & R.F.A. 2 " "	
			To England Candidates for Commissions. 3 " "	
			" " " Leave 48 " "	
			From " " " 72 " "	
			Admissions to Hospital 7 " "	
			Rejoined from Hospital 15 " "	

Army Form C. 2118.

WAR DIARY
or
INTELLIGENCE SUMMARY.
(Erase heading not required.)

Instructions regarding War Diaries and Intelligence Summaries are contained in F. S. Regs., Part II. and the Staff Manual respectively. Title pages will be prepared in manuscript.

Place	Date	Hour	Summary of Events and Information	Remarks and references to Appendices
BUS	31/7		18 - 180st Amsⁿ Wagons with General Horses are Proceed to Clay Quarry. Sheet 57c V.3.c.d. for attachment to 59th Div^l Artillery —	08.1
			The following Arrivals and Departures for the month note:—	
			Posted from R.H. & R.F.A Base Depot. 115 other ranks.	
			" " 211th Brigade R.F.A 3 " " "	
			" " To 210th Brigade " 39 " " "	
			" " 211th " " 70 " " "	
			" " Base. R.H. & R.F.A. 2 " " "	
			To England Candidates for Commissions. 3 " " "	
			" " Leave 48 " " "	
			" " " " 72 " " "	
			Admissions to Hospital 7 " " "	
			Returned from Hospital 15 " " "	

Vol 5

CONFIDENTIAL

WAR DIARY

— OF —

42ND DIVISIONAL AMMUNITION COLUMN.

From 1-6-17   To 30-6-17

VOLUME 3

42 Divisional Ammunition Column, R.F.A.
WAR DIARY or INTELLIGENCE SUMMARY

Army Form C. 2118.

Place	Date	Hour	Summary of Events and Information	Remarks and references to Appendices
Buc	30/4/17	—	Distribution of Unit. H.Q. and A. Echelon Sheet 57c. O. 24. B. Echelon O. 27.	
"	2.6.17	—	2/Lt. D.T. McKenzie posted to A/211 Brigade. R.F.A.	A.S.2.
"	"	—	" H.B. Gibbs A/211 Brigade posted to No 2 Section	
"	8.6.17	—	" S.F. Hayward attached, pending 42 T.M.B?	
"	19.6.17	—	" E.G. Walker attached to 210th Bde R.F.A.	
"	26.6.17	—	" L.S. Dale joined and posted to No 3 Section	
"	"	—	" F.C. Woodward attached to 210th Bde R.F.A.	A.S.1.
"	"	—	" A.W. Hame posted to X/42 T.M. Battery	
"	30.6.17		The following arrivals and departures for the month viz.	
			Posted from R.H. & R.F.A. Base. 143 O.R.'s	
			" " 210th Bde 1 "	
			" " 211 " 2 "	
			Sent to 210th 43 "	
			" " 211 " 97 "	
			" " Base 6 "	
			To England Candidate for Commission 3 "	
			" " on leave 48 "	
			Rejoined from leave 57 "	
			Admissions to Hospital 37 "	
			Rejoined from Hospital	

A.S. Beigge Lt Col.
Commanding 42 D.A. Column

CONFIDENTIAL

WAR DIARY

— OF —

42nd DIVISIONAL AMMUNITION COLUMN

FROM 1.7.17 TO 31.7.17

VOLUME 3.

WAR DIARY
or 42nd Divisional Ammunition Column R.F.A
INTELLIGENCE SUMMARY.

(Erase heading not required.)

Army Form C. 2118.

Place	Date	Hour	Summary of Events and Information	Remarks and references to Appendices
Bus.	3.7.17		Distribution of unit. H.Q and "A" Echelon SHEET 57c O.24. "B" Echelon G.13.t "B" Echelon, proceeded by route march to "ACHIET-LE-PETIT, SHEET 57c G.13t ROUTE:- BUS - BIHUCOURT - DUROUITE LE HAIE - GOMIECOURT - BAPAUME	A.E.1
	10.7.17		Lieut R. HARTLEY, attached to A/210 Bde R.F.A	
	10.7.17		2nd Lt V. WARE, attached from A/210 Bde R.F.A	
	13.7.17		2nd Lt G.F. ADAMS joined on posted to No 1 Section.	A.1.1
	23.7.17		2nd Lt A.W. HAME detached to join 42nd T.M Bs.	
	27.7.17		Captain A. MIGHTON posted to D/210 Bde R.F.A	
	29.7.17		2nd Lt T.M.F. RABET, posted to No 2 Section	
			Lieut L. Buck, attached to "N" Anti-Aircraft Battery	
	31.7.17		The arrivals and departures for the month were:-	A.3.1
			Joined from R.M.V. R.F.A Base Depot — 12 O.Rs	
			Posted to 210th Bde R.F.A — 3 O.Rs	
			Posted to 42nd T.M Batteries — 12 "	
			Posted to Base (pending discharge) — 1 "	
			Admissions to Hospital — 24 "	
			Rejoined from Hospital — 17 "	
			To FORWARD on leave — 142 "	
			Rejoined from leave — 75 "	

A.E. Wright Lieut Colonel
Commanding 42nd D.A.C.

Vol 7

CONFIDENTIAL

WAR DIARY
of
42nd D.A.C.

From 1-8-17 to 31-8-17.

Vol VI.

Army Form C. 2118.

WAR DIARY
or
INTELLIGENCE SUMMARY.
(Erase heading not required.)

42nd Div. Amm. Column R.F.A.

Place	Date	Hour	Summary of Events and Information	Remarks and references to Appendices
POPERINGHE	31.8.17		DISTRIBUTION OF UNIT :- H.QRS. A & B ECHELONS Sheet 28 G.17 a 9.4	
BUS	1.8.17		2nd Lieut. L.S. DALE posted to 84th Brigade R.F.A.	A.S.1
"	15.8.14		Captain C.H.G. PHILP R.A.M.C. ceased to perform duties of M.O. to 42nd D.A.C.	A.S.2
"	15.8.14		Captain R.A. McKAY R.A.M.C. assumed duties of M.O. and Captain PHILP	
ACHIET-LE-PETIT	21.8.17		"B" Echelon proceeded by road and entrained at ALBERT & detrained at	A.S.P.
GODEWAERSVELDE	22.8.17		"B" Echelon detrained and proceeded by road via ABEELE to WATOU Sheet 27 K.10.d	
BUS	25.8.14		No. 1 Section proceeded by road and entrained at BAPAUME	A.S.3
"	26.8.17		" " " " " " " " PERONNE	A.S.4
"			No. 2 HEAD QUARTERS " " BAPAUME	
GODEWAERSVELDE	28.8.14		No. 2 Section detrained and proceeded by road via ABEELE to WATOU Sheet 27 K.10.d	A.S.P.
FROM GN	26.8.17		No. 1 " " " " " " " WATOU	
WATOU	27.8.17		HEAD QUARTERS " " " " " " HILLHOEK, HOPOUTRE and BOSSEBOOM to where 13th DAC	
	29.8.17		H.QRS. A & B ECHELONS proceeded by road via HILLHOEK, HOPOUTRE and BOSSEBOOM to where 13th DAC	
			at G.17, a 9.4. Sheet 29.4	
	31.8.17		The arrivals and departures during the month were:-	
			Proceeded on leave to U.K. 86 O.Rs.	
			Rejoined from leave to U.K. 1 Officer & 136 O.Rs.	
			Evacuated to Hospital 27 O.Rs	
			Rejoined from Hospital 17 O.Rs	
			Posted to Base Depot 3 O.Rs	
			Posted from other units 2 O.Rs	A.S.2
			Posted to 210th Bde RFA 5 O.Rs	
			Posted to 211th Bde RFA 6 O.Rs	

31.8.1917

A.S. Gillespie
Lieut. Colonel
Commanding 42nd D.A.C.

CONFIDENTIAL

WAR DIARY

of

42nd D.A.C.

From 1-9-17 to 30-9-17.

Vol VII.

WAR DIARY or **INTELLIGENCE SUMMARY**
(Erase heading not required.)

Army Form C. 2118.

42ⁿᵈ Divisional Ammunition Column

Place	Date	Hour	Summary of Events and Information	Remarks and references to Appendices
POPERINGHE	1-9-17		DISTRIBUTION OF UNIT: H.QRS, A & B. ECHELONS. Sheet 28. G.17.a.9.4.	
"	7-9-17		2ⁿᵈ Lieut. A.W. HAMS. Posted from H2ⁿᵈ T.M. B5.	
"	8-9-17		Captain. T.A. HIGHAM, attached 210ᵗʰ Brigade R.F.A.	
"	9-9-17		Captain. G.W. MARRS. attached from 211ᵗʰ Brigade, assumes command of Nº 1 Section	A.S.1
"	12-9-17		One other rank. Died from "Shell Gas Poisoning"	
"	18-9-17		2ⁿᵈ Lieut. T.A. STUTTARD Posted to Nº 3 Section Hq Nº 3 Section	
"	19-9-17		2ⁿᵈ Lieut. T. KNOWLES Posted from Nº 3 Section from Base	
"	— —		2ⁿᵈ Lieut. G.F. BICK, Posted to Nº 1 Section from Base	
"	— —		Lieut. M.L. SOUNSBY Posted from 291 ˢᵗ Brigade R.F.A.	
"	25-9-17		One other rank "Killed in Action"	
"	26-9-17		Lieut. H.S. SMALLMAN, Posted to Nº 1 Section from Base	
"	— —		2ⁿᵈ Lieut. W. WARD " " Nº 2 " " "	
"	— —		2ⁿᵈ Lieut. F.T. BLENNERHASSETT, " " Nº 3 " " "	
"	29-9-17		Lieut. H.S. SMALLMAN Posted to 210ᵗʰ Brigade from Nº 1 Section	
"	30-9-17		H.QRS, A & B ECHELONS, Procession by road via POPERINGHE, ST. JAN - TER BIEZEN, HOUTKERQUE, and HERZEELE to WORMHOUDT. Sheet 27.	A.S.2
			The arrivals and departures for the month, were:—	
			Admissions to Hospital Sick — 2 Officers 15 O.R's	
			do do Wounded — 8 O.R's	
			Rejoined from Hospitals — 12 O.Rs	
			Posted from Base Depot — 192 O.Rs	
			Posted to 210ᵗʰ Brigade R.F.A. — 124 O.Rs	
			Posted to 211 " " — 73 O.Rs	
			Posted to other units — 6 O.Rs	
			Proceeded on leave to U.K. — 32 O.Rs	
			Rejoined from " " — 36 O.Rs	

30-9-1917

A.S. Collipp Lieut. Colonel
Commanding 42ⁿᵈ D.A.C.

CONFIDENTIAL

WAR DIARY

of

42nd D.A.C.

From Oct 1st 1917
To Oct 31st 1917.

Vol. VIII.

CONFIDENTIAL

October 1917

WAR DIARY
or
INTELLIGENCE SUMMARY.
(Erase heading not required.)

Army Form C. 2118.

42nd Div. Amm. Column.

Ref⁼ 1/40,000 FURNES MAP (Provisional)

Place	Date	Hour	Summary of Events and Information	Remarks and references to Appendices
WORMHOUDT TETEGHEM	1-10-17		Head Quarters, A & B Echelons proceeded by road via WYLDER to TETEGHEM. Shut Dunkerque 1A.	
	2-10-17		Head Quarters, A & B Echelons proceeded by route via UXAM GHYVELDE ADINKERKE to COXYDE X 7.d.2.8. Sh.7. 1/40,000.	
COXYDE	3-10-17		Duplication of units. H.Qrs. X 7.d. 2.B. N°1 Section X 7.a.2.6. N°2 Section X 7.a.3.4. BECMBERG W.17. C.4.7. FURNES. Lieut. T.W. WALMSLEY, 2nd Lieut. V.A. STUTTARD, 2nd Lieut. G.F. BICK, 2nd Lieut. W. WARD, Lieut. F.G. WOODWARD, Lieut. R. HARTLEY. Lieut. S.G. WEBBER, C.P. HUMPHREYS all posted to 210th Brigade R.F.A.	
	4-10-17		2nd Lieut. C.P. HUMPHREYS, 2nd Lieut. J.C. BORTHWICK and 2nd Lieut. G.C. WILLCOX posted from Base Depot.	
	6-10-17		Lieut. A. BUCK, 2nd Lieut. E.P. HUMPHREY, 2nd Lieut. J.C. BORTHWICK to 210th Brigade R.F.A., 2nd Lieut. F.K. BRENNERHASSETT posted to 211th Bde.	
	7-10-17		2nd Lieut. G.C. WILLCOX posted to 42nd Trench Mortar Brigade.	
	9-10-17		2nd Lieut. J.A. SHERRY posted from Base Depot.	
	10-10-17		Employment. J.A. HIGHAM posted to 310th Brigade R.F.A. Captain G.W. MARRS posted from 211th Brigade R.F.A.	
	14-10-17		2nd Lieuts W.N. CRYER, J.A. CROWL, J.D. CARRICK, S.M. COLLINS, M.A. HAMILTON and V.R. CLARKE posted from Base Depot. Head Quarters A & B Echelons proceeded & relieved 32nd D.A.C. at H.Qrs X21.c.7.8. N°1 Section X21.6.5.4.	
FURNES	16-10-17		N°2 Section X10.d.8.m. N°3 Section X21.a.2.7. Sheet "I". FURNES. 1/40,000.	
			2nd Lieuts A.W. TALBOT. W.N. CRYER and J.A. CROWL posted to 211th Brigade R.F.A.	
	18-10-17		2nd Lieuts J.D. CARRICK and S.M. COLLINS posted to 42nd Trench Mortar Brigade.	
	19-10-17		2nd Lieuts G. HAWES and M.A. PENN posted from Base Depot	
	20-10-17		2nd Lieuts T.W. MORRISS, W.M. SHELLEY, J.R. GRANT and J.R. RHODES posted from Base Depot.	
	23-10-17		2nd Lieut. T.W. MORRISS posted to 210th Brigade R.F.A., 2nd Lieuts W.M. SHELLEY and J.R. RHODES posted to 211th Brigade.	
	24-10-17		2nd Lieut. D.M. HEWITT posted from Base Depot. H.Qrs. & "B" Echelon proceeded to new camp at W.23.a.4.3 and N°1 & 2 Sections at W.21.c.5.6.	
KOKNIS PANNIS	31-10-17		Arrivals and departures during the month were as follows.	

Officers from Base Depot R.F.A. 18 Officers. 186 O.R.S.
Posted to   211th Bde. R.F.A. 1   ,,   52   ,,
    ,,   210th Bde.   11 ,,   56   ,,
    ,,   211th Bde.   6   ,,   10   ,,
    ,,   T.M. Brigade.   4   ,,   19   ,,
Admissions to Hospital.   1   ,,   14   ,,
Evacuated from Hospital.   1   ,,   14   ,,
Granted leave to U.K.   ,,   19   ,,
Evacuated from France to U.K.   ,,   14   ,,
Proceeded to U.K. as Candidate for R.A. commission. 1 ,,

A. Shipp Lieut. Colonel
Commanding 42nd D.A.C.

War Diary
of
42nd Divl Ammn Col.

From 1-11-17
To 30-11-17

Vol VIII.

Army Form C. 2118.

WAR DIARY
or
INTELLIGENCE SUMMARY.

(Erase heading not required.)

NOVEMBER 42nd Div. Amm. Column

Place	Date	Hour	Summary of Events and Information	Remarks and references to Appendices
MARKS PANNE	1-11-17		Distribution of Unit:- H.Qrs & "B" Echelon at W23.a.4.3. and 17 2 Sections at W21.a.3.6. (Karnes Provisional Stat.) 42nd Div. Amm. Column. Reorganised. "B" Echelon (No.3 Section) is now known as S.A.A Section	A.S.f.
"	4-11-17		2nd Lieut J.A. SHERRY posted to 42nd Div. T.M. Brigade.	
"	10-11-17		Capt. R.A. McKAY relinquishes appointment as M.O. and reposted to 41st Division	
"	12-11-17		Lieut. C.H. HARVEY, v.s. A.V.C. posted to No.2 Section.	
"	12-11-17		Lieut. T. MARLAND posted to H.Qrs. 42nd D.A.C. and assumes duties of M.O. vice Capt McKay	
"	17-11-17		H.Qrs. 1, 2, & S.A.A. Sections proceeded by road to GHYVELDE	
"	21-11-17			
GHYVELDE	23-11-17		H.Qrs. 1, 2, & S.A.A. Sections proceeded by road to WORMHOUDT.	
WORMHOUDT	24-11-17		H.Qrs. 1, 2, & S.A.A. Sections proceeded by road to ZERMEZEELE	
ZERMEZEELE	25-11-17		H.Qrs. 1, 2, & S.A.A. Sections proceeded by road to ST MARIE CAPPEL	
ST MARIE CAPPEL	26-11-17		H.Qrs. 1, 2, & S.A.A. Sections proceeded by road to QUESNOY	
QUESNOY	29-11-17		S.A.A. proceeded by road to relieve S.A.A Section 23rd D.A.C. at LE QUESNOY	A.S.f.
"	30-11-17		H.Qrs. 1 & 2 Sections proceeded by road to ROBECQ.	
			The undermentioned were the arrivals and departures during the month:-	
			Enlist. from Base. 6 Officer	
			Enlist. from 210th Brigade R.F.A. 21 O.Rs	
			Posted to 210th " " 10 O.Rs	
			Posted from 2.11.74 26 O.Rs	
			Posted to " 2 O.Rs	
			Posted from 2.11.74 10 O.Rs	
			Posted to 42nd T.M. Brigade 16 O.Rs	
			Posted to Base Depot 74 O.Rs	
			Proceeded on leave to U.K. 10 Officer 28 O.Rs	
			Returned from leave to U.K. 1 " 20 O.Rs	
			Admitted to Hospital 2 Officers 22 O.Rs	
			Rejoined from Hospital 8 O.Rs	

A.S. Sharpe Lieut. Colonel
Commanding 42nd D.A.C.

Confidential

War Diary
of
42nd Div. Amm. Column.

WAR DIARY
or
INTELLIGENCE SUMMARY

Army Form C. 2118.

42nd Div. Amm. Column

Vol II

DECEMBER

Place	Date	Hour	Summary of Events and Information	Remarks and references to Appendices
RUBECQ	1.12.14		Distribution of Unit :- H.Qrs. 1 & 2 Sections at RUBECQ. S.A.A. Section at LA QUESNOY. H.Qrs. & No 2 Section bivouacs by road to where 25th Divisn. as follows: H.Qrs. at W.23.c.9.1., No 1 Section at W.18.a.2.6., and No 2 Section at W.18.d.5.4., all Sheet:- BETHUNE (rembrai).	
BETHUNE	1.12.14		Lieut. T. MARLAND No 2 Section admitted to Hospital.	
"	3.12.14		2nd Lieut. E.N. JAMES posted from Base to No 1 Section.	A.S.L.
"	"		2nd Lieut. G. FRASER posted to 210th Brigade R.F.A.	
"	"		" D.M. HEWITT posted to 210th Brigade R.F.A.	
"	"		" T. KNOWLES posted to 211th Brigade R.F.A.	
"	16.12.14		Lieut. T.M. WALMSLEY, posted from 210th Brigade to No 1 Section.	
"	"		Lieut. H.B. ADAMS, posted from 211th Brigade R.F.A.	
"	"		2nd Lieut. E.N. JAMES, posted to 210th Brigade R.F.A.	
"	"		" H.L. PENN, posted to 211th Brigade R.F.A.	
"	"		" J.R. RHODES, posted to 211th Brigade R.F.A.	
"	"		The undermentioned went the arrivals and departures during the month	
"	"		Posted from Base Depot.	36. O.R.s
"	"		Posted from 210th Brigade R.F.A.	1 Officer 2. O.R.s
"	"		Posted from 211th Brigade R.F.A.	1 Officer. 1 O.R.
"	"		Posted from 42nd T.M. Brigade.	6. O.R.s
"	"		Posted to 210th Brigade R.F.A.	4 Officers 2 O.R.S.
"	"		Posted to 211th Brigade R.F.A.	2 Officers. 14. O.R.s
"	"		Posted to 42nd T.M. Brigade.	23. O.R.s
"	"		Proceeded on leave to U.K.	10 Officers. 26. O.R.
"	"		Returned from leave to U.K.	31 O.R.s
"	"		Admitted to Hospital	1 Officer 7 O.R.s
"	"		Returned from Hospital	3 O.R.s

A.E. Phillipps Lieut. Colonel
Commanding 42nd D.A.C.

CONFIDENTIAL Vol 12

WAR. DIARY
OF
42ⁿᵈ DIV. Amm. COLUMN

FROM. 1ˢᵗ JAN. 1918   TO. 1ˢᵗ FEB. 1918

VOLUMN. XIII

WAR DIARY or **INTELLIGENCE SUMMARY.**

Army Form C. 2118.

42nd Div. Amm Column

January 1918

Place	Date	Hour	Summary of Events and Information	Remarks and references to Appendices
BETHUNE	1-1-18	—	Distribution of unit :— Hd. Qrs. at W.23.c.9.1., No 1 Section at W.18.a.2.6., No 2 Section at W.18.d.5.7., S.A.A. Section at F.B. b.9.1., at BETHUNE (ambulance) Stub.	A.S.2
"	1-1-18		2nd/Lieut. W.R. ANDREWS posted from R.A.1 R.F.A. Base Depot	
"	3-1-18		Lieut. H.B. ADAMS posted to Yorkshire Divisional ROUEN, as Assistant Instr Combt Officer.	
"	12-1-18		Lieut. J.J. COWIESON posted to 211th Bde R.F.A	
"	12-1-18		2nd/Lieut. M.A. HAMILTON posted to 210th Bde R.F.A.	
"	12-1-18		Lieut. G.H. COOPER, posted from 210th Bde R.F.A.	
"	18-1-18		Lieut. L. BUCK posted from 211th Bde R.F.A.	
"	31-1-18		2nd/Lieut. T.W. MORRIS posted from 210th Bde R.F.A.	A.S.4
			Other undermentioned were the arrivals and departures during the month :—	
			Posted from R.M.4 R.F.A. Base Depot. 1 Officer 62 O.Rs	
			Posted to 210th Brigade R.F.A. 1 Officer 35 O.Rs	
			Posted to 211th Brigade R.F.A. 1 Officer 23 O.Rs	
			Posted from 210th Brigade R.F.A. 2 Officers 9 O.Rs	
			Posted from 211th Brigade R.F.A. 1 Officer 8 O.Rs	
			Posted from R.A. H. Qrs. R.F.A. 2 O.Rs	
			Posted to Yorkshire Directorate ROUEN 1 Officer 20 O.Rs	
			Posted to 2nd T.M. Brigade 67 O.Rs	
			Proceeded on leave to U.K. 2 Officers 41 O.Rs	
			Returned from leave to U.K. 2 Officers 5 O.Rs	
			Admitted to Hospital. 4 O.Rs	
			Returned from Hospital. 2 Officers	

A. Spring Lieut. Colonel
Commanding 42nd D.A.C.

WD 13

CONFIDENTIAL

WAR DIARY

OF

42nd DIV. AMM. COLUMN

FROM 1-2-18.   TO 28-2-18.

VOLUMN XIII

FEBRUARY 1918   VOLUME XIV

Army Form C. 2118.

WAR DIARY
or
INTELLIGENCE SUMMARY
(Erase heading not required.)

42nd Div. Amm. Column

Instructions regarding War Diaries and Intelligence Summaries are contained in F.S. Regs., Part II. and the Staff Manual respectively. Title pages will be prepared in manuscript.

Place	Date	Hour	Summary of Events and Information	Remarks and references to Appendices
BETHUNE	1.2.18		Distribution of Units :- H. Qrs W.23.c.9.1., No.1 Section at W.18 a.2.6., No.2 Section at W.18 d.5.7. S.A.A. Section at F.8. b.9.7. all BETHUNE (Combrin) Sheet.	
"	6.2.18		Sent G.S. Rivett-Carnac polo from Base.	A.S.2
"	14.2.18		S.A.A. Section proceeded by Rail to VENDIN-LEZ-BETHUNE (W.26.d.3.3) BETHUNE (Combrin) Sheet.	
"	16.2.18		H.Qrs, No.1 Section and No.2 Section proceeded by way to GONNEHEM to camps situated at V.17.d.7.7. V.23.b.8.8. and V.18.c. 25.9a. respectively. BETHUNE (Combrin) Sheet. on relief by 55th Divisional Ammunition Column.	A.S.?

The undermentioned were the arrivals and departures during the month.

	OFFICERS	OTHER RANKS
A.S. Clegg		33.
Posted from R.H. & R.F.A. Base Depot.		12
Posted to 210th Brigade R.F.A.		21
Posted to 211th Brigade R.F.A.		27.
Posted from 42nd T.M. Brigade	1	22
Proceeded on leave to U.K.	2	34
Rejoined from leave to U.K.	1	12
Admitted to Hospital		15
Rejoined from Hospital		5
Posted to R.H. & R.F.A. Base Depot		1
Transferred to A.V.C.		1
Transferred to R.F.C.		1
Posted to 42nd T.M. Brigade		11

A.S. Clegg
Lieut. Colonel
Commanding 42nd D.A.C.

42nd Divisional Artillery

42nd DIVISIONAL AMMUNITION COLUMN R.F.A.

MARCH 1918

Vol 14

Confidential

WAR DIARY.

OF

42nd DIV AMM COLUMN.

VOL. XV

From 1/3/18. To 31/3/18

R.O.

MARCH 1918. VOLUME XI

WAR DIARY
or
INTELLIGENCE SUMMARY.

Army Form C. 2118.

(Erase heading not required.)

42nd Div. Amm. Column

Place	Date	Hour	Summary of Events and Information	Remarks and references to Appendices
GONNEHEM	1-3-18		Distribution of Unit:- H.Qrs V.17.d.77., No1 Section V.23.b & 8., No 2 Section, V.18.c.25.90 and S.A.A. Section W.26.d.3.3. all BETHUNE (Cambrin) Sheet.	1918
"	3-3-18		S.A.A. Section proceeded to new camp at V.18.a central. BETHUNE (Cambrin) Sheet.	
"	26-3-18		Major H.K. BARNES M.C. posted from 11th Brigade R.F.A. and assumed command of 42nd D.A.C. vice Lieut. Colonel A.E. JOBLIFFE, V.D.	
"	23-3-18		Lieut Colonel A.E. JOBLIFFE, V.D., proceeded to U.K. to report at WAR OFFICE	
"	23-3-18		H.Qrs, No 1, 2, & S.A.A Section proceeded by road to GAUCHEN-LEGAL	
GAUCHEN LEGAL	26-3-18		H.Qrs, No 1, 2 & S.A.A Section proceeded by road to BIENVILLERS-au-Bois	
BIENVILLERS au Bois	25-3-18		H.Qrs, No 1, 2, & S.A.A Section proceeded by road to set between AYETTE & BUCQUOY	
	25-3-18	7·am	S.A.A. Section delivered to sit at 6:05 a.m R.F.A.	
AYETTE	26-3-18		H.Qrs No 1 & 2 Sections proceeded to camp roadside GAUDIEMPRÉ	
ESSARTS	26-3-18		S.A.A Section proceeded to camp roadside of BIENVILLERS-au-Bois	
	26-3-18		2nd Lieut J.W. REYNOLDS posted from "D" Battery 211th Brigade to No 1 Section D.A.C.	
BIENVILLERS au Bois	27-3-18		S.A.A. Section proceeded to camp located at HENU	
	31-3-18		Distribution of Unit:- H Qrs, No 1 & 2 Sections at GAUDIEMPRÉ and S.A.A Section at HENU.	1918

The undermentioned were the arrivals and departures during the month.

Posted from 11th Brigade R.F.A. — 1 OFFICER 2 O.Rs
Proceeded to U.K. on leave — 1 OFFICER
Posted from 211th Brigade R.F.A. — 1 OFFICER
Posted to 211th Brigade R.F.A. —
Posted to 211th Brigade R.F.A. — 20 O.Rs
                                   30 O.Rs
Proceeded on leave to U.K. — 2 OFFICERS 14 O.Rs
Reported from leave to U.K. — 1 OFFICER 15 O.Rs
Admitted to Hospital — 1 O.R
Discharged from Hospital to Unit — 4 O.Rs

H.K. Barnes Major
Commanding 42nd D.A.C.

IV. Corps.
Third Army.

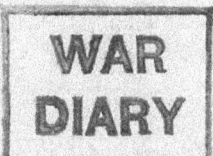

42nd DIVISIONAL AMMUNITION COLUMN.

A P R I L

1 9 1 8

Vol 15

CONFIDENTIAL

WAR DIARY

OF

42ⁿᵈ DIV. AMM. COLUMN

FROM. 1ST. APRIL. 1918.   TO. 30TH. APRIL. 1918.

VOL. XVI

APRIL 1918

WAR DIARY
or
INTELLIGENCE SUMMARY
(Erase heading not required.)

Army Form C. 2118.

VOLUME XVI
42nd Div. Amm Column

Place	Date	Hour	Summary of Events and Information	Remarks and references to Appendices
GAUDIEMPRÉ SOUASTRE	1-4-18		HQrs. Nº 1 & 2 Sections proceeded by road via ST. AMAND, to relieve 62nd D.A.C. at SOUASTRE.	HKB
—	5-4-18		2nd Lieut. P. CHAPMAN, posted from 79th Bde R.F.A.	
—	8-4-18		S.A.A. Section joined main body of Column at SOUASTRE from HÉNU.	
—	9-4-18		2nd Lieut F. STANNARD posted from 41st D.A.C.	
—	12-4-18		2nd Lieut W.R. ANDREWS, Wounded in action, remained at duty	
—	15-4-18		Lieut. A.M. COOPER, 2nd Lieut. A.M. BREMNER and P. CHAPMAN, posted to 210th Brigade R.F.A.	
—	16-4-18		2nd Lieut. V.R. CLARKE, posted to 211th Brigade R.F.A.	
—	17-4-18		S.A.A. Section proceeded to relieve S.A.A. Section, 62nd D.A.C. at COUIN. (J.I. b.5.7. Sheet 57↓)	
—	17-4-18		2nd Lieut. J.R. RHODES, posted to R.H. & R.F.A. Base Depot, LE HAVRE. Auth: D.G.M.S. G.H.Q. Nº 445/14/9/1917	
—	18-4-18		H.Qrs. Nº 1 & 2 Sections proceeded to relieve H.Qrs., Nº 1 & 2 Sections, 62nd D.A.C. at COUIN. (Camp 55 located at J.1. d.9.0, J.2.C.2.2 and J.2.C.7.7 respectively. Sheet 57↓)	
COUIN	23-4-18		Lieut. F. STANNARD, posted to 7th D.A.C.	HKB
			Lieut. L. BUCK, admitted to Hospital. (Sick. P.U.O.)	
			The undermentioned were the arrivals and departures during the month	
			Posted from 41st D.A.C. — 1 Officer, 1 O.R.	
			Posted from 79th Bde R.F.A. — 1 Officer	
			Posted from R.H. & R.F.A. Base Depot —	
			Posted from 211th Bde. R.F.A. — 195 O.Rs	
			Rejoined from Hospital — 3 O.Rs	
			Rejoined from Leave to U.K. — 7 O.Rs	
			Posted to 41st D.A.C. — 1 Officer, 480 O.Rs, 1 D.R.	
			Posted to 4 7th D.A.C. — 1 Officer	
			Posted to R.H. & R.F.A. Base Depot — 1 Officer	
			Posted to 210th Brigade R.F.A — 3 Officers, 53 O.Rs	
			Posted to 211th Brigade R.F.A — 1 Officer, 98 O.Rs	
			Admitted to Hospital — 1 Officer, 9.17 O.Rs	

H.K. Browne Major
Commanding 42nd D.A.C.

Vol 16

Confidential

War Diary

of

42nd Div. Amm. Column.

From 1st May 1918.   To 31st May 1918.

Volume XVII

WAR DIARY or INTELLIGENCE SUMMARY

Army Form C. 2118.

MAY 1918   **VOLUME XVII**

42nd D.H. Amn Column

Place	Date	Hour	Summary of Events and Information	Remarks and references to Appendices
COUIN	1-5-18		Distribution of unit:- H.Qrs, T.1. d.9.0., N°1 Section, T.2.c.2.2., N°2 Section, T.2.c.7.7., S.A.A. Section, T.1.b.5.7., all sheet 57d	
-"-	2-5-18		Lieut. T.T. COWLISON, posted from 211th Bde R.F.A.	
-"-	3-5-18		2nd Lieut. J.A. SHERRY, posted to 211th Bde R.F.A.	
-"-	6-5-18		S.A.A. Section moved to camp, located at T.8.a.9.2. (Sheet 57d)	
-"-	9-5-18		B.A.A. Section moved to camp, located at C.17.a.8.8. (Sheet 57d).	
-"-	11-5-18		Capt. H.E. BEARD, posted to 211th Brigade R.F.A.	
-"-	11-5-18		Lieut. G. STEPHENSON, posted from Base Depot	
-"-	12-5-18		Lieut. T. HARLAND, admitted to Hospital (Sick).	
-"-	25-5-18		Lieut. G. STEPHENSON, posted to 211th Bde R.F.A.	
-"-	27-5-18		2nd Lieut. J.W. TINDGAH, and 2nd Lieut F.P.W. BOWLES, M.C., M.M., posted from Base Depot. 2nd Lieut. J.W. TINDGAH, posted to 210th Bde R.F.A., and 2nd Lieut F.P.W. BOWLES, M.C., M.M. posted to 211th Bde.	/AB3
			The undermentioned were the arrivals + departures for the month.	
			Posted from Indian R.A. Rein Base Depot 3 Officers 150 O.R's.	
			Posted from R.H. + R.F.A. Base Depot 293 O.R's	
			Posted from R.A. H.Qrs 42nd D.H. 3 O.R's	
			Posted from 211th Brigade R.F.A. 1 Officer 1 O.R.	
			Rejoined from Hospital 8 O.R's	
			Admitted to Hospital 1 Officer 24 O.R's (Includes 14 to Venn Hospital)	
			Posted to 210th Brigade R.F.A. 1 Officer 116 O.R's.	
			Posted to 211th Brigade R.F.A. 4 Officers 159 O.R's	
			Posted to 312th Brigade R.F.A. 1 O.R.	

J.C. Crowned, Major.
Commanding 42nd D.A.C.

Vol. 17

WAR DIARY.
of
42nd DIV. Amm. Column.

From 1/6/18 To 30-6-18

Vol. XVIII

Army Form C. 2118.

WAR DIARY
or
INTELLIGENCE SUMMARY.
(Erase heading not required.)

42nd Div. Amm. Column
Volume XVIII
June 1918

Place	Date	Hour	Summary of Events and Information	Remarks and references to Appendices
COLIN	1.6.18		Distribution of Units. H.Qrs. J.1.d.9.0. No.1 Section, J.2.c.2.2, No.2 Section, J.2.c.7.9. and S.A.A. Section. C.17.a.8.8. all Sheet 57P.	MA3
-.-	9.6.18		S.A.A. Section moved to camp located at J.20.c.1.9. Sheet 57P. Lieut. T. HARLAND rejoined unit from Hospital	
-.-	23.6.19		Lieut. T. HARLAND attached to 211th Brigade R.F.A.	
			The undermentioned were the assumts and departures during the month:-	
				O.	O.R.
			Posted from R.H. & R.F.A. Base Depot.	0.	119.
			Posted from Indian R.A. Advance Base Depot	-	17.
			Posted to do do do		15.
			Posted to 210th Brigade R.F.A.		44.
			Posted to 211th Brigade R.F.A.		81
			Posted to 42nd Trench Mortar Brigade		10.
			Admissions to Hospital (Europeans)		34.
			do do do (Indians)		5
			Rejoined from Hospital (Europeans)	1	15
			do do do (Indians)		3
			Proceeded on leave to U.K.		4
			Rejoined from leave to U.K.		1

H.K. Bernard Major R.F.A.
Commanding 42nd D.A.C.

MKB

Vol 16

CONFIDENTIAL

WAR DIARY
OF
42ⁿᵈ DIV. AMM. COLUMN

From. 1/7/18.   To. 31/7/18.

VOL. XIX

WAR DIARY or INTELLIGENCE SUMMARY

42nd Div. Amm. Column

Volume XIX

July 1918.

Place	Date	Hour	Summary of Events and Information	Remarks and references to Appendices
COUIN.	1-7-18		Distribution of Units:- Head Qrs. T.1.d.9.0., No.1 Section, T.2.c.2.2., No.2 Section, T.2.c.7.9. and S.A.A. Section, T.20.c.1.9., all Sheet 57D.	Ap3
COUIN.	5-7-18		H. Qrs, No.1 & 2 Sections proceeded by road via BUS-LES-ARTOIS to LOUVEN COURT MAP REFERENCES H.QRS. I.35.a.8.3. No.1 Section, I.35.6.5.2, and No.2 Section, I.35.a.8.8. Sheet 57D.	
LOUVENCOURT	10-7-18		Lieut. G.T. Corkinson, 2nd Lieut. A. Young, and 2nd Lieut. A.T. Rogerson posted from Base.	
-..-	18-7-18		2nd Lieut. A. Young and 2nd Lieut. A.T. Rogerson, posted to 211th Brigade R.F.A.	
-..-	18-7-18		Lieut. E.M. Fry, C, posted from Base.	
-..-	20-7-18		Lieut. E.M. Fry, M.C. posted to 211th Brigade R.F.A.	
-..-	20-7-18		Lieut. J.E. Hughes, relinquishes rank of Acting Captain on ceasing to perform duties of Adjutant.	
-..-	21-7-18		Lieut. D.F. Mackenzie, appointed Adjutant vice Lieut. Hughes, and appointed Acting Captain.	
-..-	22-7-18		Lieut. D.F. Mackenzie, posted from A/211th Bde. R.F.A.	
-..-	24-7-18		Lieut. J.E. Hughes, posted to 210th Brigade R.F.A.	
			The undermentioned were the arrivals and departures during the month:-	Ap3
				4 Officers	145 O.Rs	Admissions to Hospital	14 O.Rs
			Posted from Base	do	do	18 O.Rs	do (Indians)	18 O.Rs
			do do (Indian Personnel)		55 O.Rs	Returned from Hospital	12 O.Rs
			Posted to 210th Bde R.F.A.	1 Officer	79 O.Rs	do do (Indians)	3 O.Rs
			Posted to 211th Bde R.F.A.	3 Officers	22 O.Rs	Posted to 59th D.A.C. (Indians)	9 O.Rs
			Posted to 42nd T.M.Bde			Posted to 59th D.A.C., 2 Officers, 12 O.Rs	
			Proceeded on Leave to U.K. 4 Officers. 29 O.Rs. Rejoined from leave to U.K., 2 Officers, 12 O.Rs				
			Posted from 211th Bde R.F.A., 1 Officer, R, and 1 O.R.				

W.C.Burnel
Major R.H.A.
Commanding 42nd D.A.C.

WD 19

War Diary

of

42ⁿᵈ Dn. Ammunition Column R.F.A.

From 1ˢᵗ August 1918 to 31ˢᵗ August 1918.

Volume XX

Army Form C. 2118.

WAR DIARY
~~INTELLIGENCE SUMMARY~~
(Erase heading not required)

42nd DIV. AMM. COLUMN.   AUGUST 1918.   VOLUME XX

Instructions regarding War Diaries and Intelligence Summaries are contained in F.S. Regs., Part II. and the Staff Manual respectively. Title pages will be prepared in manuscript.

Place	Date	Hour	Summary of Events and Information	Remarks and references to Appendices
LOUVENCOURT	1-8-18		Redistribution of unit:- H.Qrs. I.35.a.8.3, No.1 Section I.35.a.8.8. and S.A.A. Section, J.20.c.1.7. all Sheet 57d.	} A.U.3
"	2-8-18		S.A.A. Section, moved from J.20.c.1.7. (Bds.-165.-ARTOIS) to J.35.b.9.2. Sheet 57d.	
"	10-8-18		Column re-organized on W.E.818. and became composed of part British & part Indian personnel.	
"	12-8-19		Lieut. F. FITCH, 59th Divn. Ind. Rabout Bay, posted from Ind. R.A. Base Depot. ROUEN.	
"	24-8-18		H.Qrs, Nos. 1, 2 & S.A.A. Sections moved to BERTRANCOURT P.3.a. Sheet 57d.	
BERTRANCOURT	25-8-18		H.Qrs, No.1 & 2 Sections proceeded via COURCELLES-AU-BOIS, COLINCAMPS, SERRE, PUISEUX-AU-MONT and BUCQUOY to camp located at K.4. a central Sheet 57d.	} A.U.3
"	"		S.A.A. Section, proceeded via COURCELLES-AU-BOIS, and COLINCAMPS to camp located at K.32.d.4.M Sheet57d.	
BUCQUOY	26-8-18		H.Qrs, No.1 & 2 Sections, proceeded via ACHIET-LE-PETIT, PUISEUX-AU-MONT, and MIRAUMONT to camp located at K.3.B. C.H.9. Sheet 57d.	
MIRAUMONT	24-8-18		S.A.A.Section, proceeded via SERRE, MIRAUMONT, and IRLES to camp located at A.24.a.8.4. Sheet 57d =	
"	30-8-18		H.Qrs. No.1 & 2 Section, proceeded via IRLES to camp located at A.29.a. Sheet 57d.	
			The undermentioned were the arrivals and departures during the month.	
				Off. O.Rs. O.Rs
			Posted from Base	1 52 34.
			Posted to Base	4 10.
			Posted to Third Army Reinforcement Camp	18 8.
			Posted from 210th Bde R.F.A.	19 1.
			Posted to 62nd D.A.C.	38.
			Posted from 211th "	1 "
			Posted to 36th A.A. Section	4 3.
			Posted from T.M. Brigade	12 5.
			Admitted to Hospital	1/2 48.
			Rejoined from Hospital	
			Proceeded on leave to U.K.	3
			Rejoined from leave to U.K.	3

H.L. Clement
Major R.F.A.
Commanding, 42nd D.A.C.

Vol 20

Confidential

42ND DIVL. AMMUNITION COLUMN.
WAR DIARY.
VOL. XXI.
SEPTEMBER 1918

Army Form C. 2118.

Sheet No 1

SEPTEMBER WAR DIARY
1918 INTELLIGENCE SUMMARY.
(Erase heading not required.)

42nd Div. Ammunition Column

VOLUME XXI

Instructions regarding War Diaries and Intelligence Summaries are contained in F.S. Regs. Part II. and the Staff Manual respectively. Title pages will be prepared in manuscript.

Place	Date	Hour	Summary of Events and Information	Remarks and references to Appendices
GREVILLERS	1-9-18		Distribution of Unit. H.Qrs. No 1 & No 2 Sections, G.2.9.a. Sheet 57C. & S.A.A. Section G.27.a.6.4. Sheet 57C.	
"	3-9-18		H.Qrs. No 1 & 2 Sections proceeded via GREVILLERS & THILLOY & Camp at L.9.a. Sheet 57C.	
THILLOY	4-9-18		H.Qrs. No 1 & 2 Sections proceeded via BEAULENCOURT, VILLERS AU FLOS & Camp at O.13.d. Sheet 57C.	
"			S.A.A. Section proceeded via GREVILLERS to Camp at M.31.d. Sheet 57C.	
BARASTRE	7-9-18		No 2 Section proceeded via VILLERS AU FLOS to Camp at N10.a. Sheet 57C.	
"	8-9-18		H.Qrs. proceeded via VILLERS AU FLOS, BEAULENCOURT, THILLOY, GREVILLERS and IRLES to Camp at L.36.c.4.9. Sheet 57C.	
			No 2 Section proceeded via REINCOURT, BEAULENCOURT, LIGNY-THILLOY, LE BARQUE, WARLENCOURT and IRLES to Camp at L.36.c.4.9.	
MIRAUMONT	9-9-18		H.Qrs & No 2 Section proceeded via IRLES, GREVILLERS, THILLOY, BEAULENCOURT and VILLERS AU FLOS to camp at O.13.d. Sheet 57C.	
BARASTRE	22-9-18		S.A.A. Section proceeded via THILLOY, BEAULENCOURT, VILLERS AU FLOS, and HAPLINCOURT to Camp at VELU, J.25.d.1.1. Sheet 57C.	
"	24-9-18		No 2 Section proceeded via BARASTRE to Camp at O.18.central. Sheet 57C.	
"	25-9-18		H.Qrs & No 1 Section proceeded via BARASTRE & BERTINCOURT to Camp at P.14.f.5.4. Sheet 57C.	
BERTINCOURT	27-9-18		No 2 Section moved to P.9.C.	

Departures {
The undermentioned were this arrivals & departures of Officers during month.
Capt. F. SOWLER admitted to Hospital, Sick 19.9.18.
Capt. A.S.E. RICHARDS admitted to Hospital G.S.W. (Slight) 29.9.18.
}

Arrivals {
CAPT. E. NUTTALL, posted from Base Depot to S.A.A. Section, 21.9.18.
2/LT. T.P. HEYWORTH posted from Base Depot to S.A.A. Section, 21.9.18. Attached 42nd R.A H.Q. from 21/9/18
CAPT. A.S.E. RICHARDS posted from Base Depot to S.A.A. Section, 25.9.18.
LT. E.R. KNOX, posted from Base Depot to No 2 Section, 13.9.18. Attached IV Corps H.Q from 13/9/18.
2/LT. F. HETHERINGTON posted from Base Depot to No 1 Section, 29.9.18.
2/LT. T. MITKEN " " " " " No 2 Section 29.9.18.
4 Officers proceeded on leave to U.K. & 3 Officers returned from leave to U.K.
}

Continued.

Sheet 2

WAR DIARY *or* **INTELLIGENCE SUMMARY**

Army Form C. 2118.

SEPTEMBER 1918.

42ND DIVISIONAL AMMN COLUMN

VOLUME XXI continued

Place	Date	Hour	Summary of Events and Information	Remarks and references to Appendices
			The undermentioned were the arrivals + departures of O.R.s during month	
			Posted from Base (British) 111 — Posted to 42nd D.A.H.Q. 54	Ann
			— do — (Indian) 5 — Posted to 210 Brigade R.F.A. 57	
			Posted from 211 Bde. R.F.A. 2 — Posted to 211 Brigade R.F.A.	
			Posted from 42nd T.M.B. 1 — 26 + 293 A.F.A. Bde Reinforcements	
			Posted from 26th A.F.A. Bde. 1 — attached 42nd D.A.C. posted to 211 Bde. 11	
			Returned from Leave to U.K. 69 — Indian O.R.s admitted to Hospital 4	
			Posted from 42nd R.A.H.Q. 2 — (Accidental injury)	
				Indian O.R.s Killed 1
				do do wounded – to Hospital 1
				do do sick – do 1
				British do sick – do 2
				Proceeded on Leave to U.K. 93
	1-10-18			

Signed, Capt
Commanding 42nd D.A.C.

Confidential.

War Diary

of

2nd Divisional Ammunition Column.

From 1st October, 1918. To 31st October, 1918.

Volume XXII

Army Form C. 2118.

SHEET No. 1. 42nd Div. Amm. Column.

WAR DIARY or INTELLIGENCE SUMMARY.

(Erase heading not required.)

VOLUME XXV.

OCTOBER 1918.

Instructions regarding War Diaries and Intelligence Summaries are contained in F. S. Regs., Part II. and the Staff Manual respectively. Title pages will be prepared in manuscript.

Place	Date	Hour	Summary of Events and Information	Remarks and references to Appendices
BERTINCOURT	1-10-18		Distribution of Unit:- Head Qrs. & No 1 Section, P. 14. b. 8. 4., No 2 Section P. 9. c. and S.A.A. Section I. 25. d. 1. 1. all Sheet 57.c	
—	1-10-18		Head Qrs, Nos 1, & 2 Sections proceeded via METZ to camps located at Head Qrs, Q. 10. c. 3. 9 and Nos 1 & 2 Sections at Q. 10. a. Sheet 57.c	
TRESCAULT	2-10-18		2nd Lieuts F. HETHERINGTON and J. AITKEN, posted to 210th Bde. R.F.A. 2nd Lieut. J.P. HEYWORTH, posted to 211th Bde RFA.	
—	8-10-18		Captain E. NUTTALL, posted to 211th Bde. R.F.A., Captain C.I. SCOWCROFT posted from 211th Bde R.F.A.	WR3
—	9-10-18		2nd Lieut. W.R. ANDREWS, admitted to Hospital "Sick"	
—	8-10-18		S.A.A. Section, moved to camp located at Q. 15. d. 9. 2. Sheet 57.c	
—	9-10-18		Head Qrs, Nos 1, & 2 Sections, proceeded via RIBECOURT, MARCOING, LE BOSQUET, LES RUES-DES-VIGNES and LESDAIN to camps at N.2.C. Sheet 57.B	
—	10-10-18		S.A.A. Section, proceeded (by same route as H.Qrs, 1 & 2 Sections) to camp at M.5.c.1.2. Sheet 57.B	
ESNES	11-10-18		Head Qrs 1 & 2 Sections proceeded via LONGSART, and FONTAINE to camp at I. 9. c. 9. 5. and S.A.A. Section to camp at H. 33. b. all Sheet 57.B	
BEAUVOIS	12-10-18		S.A.A. Section moved to camp located at I. 15. b. 3. 8. Sheet 57.B	
—	15-10-18		Head Qrs. Nos 1, 2, & S.A.A. Sections moved to camps located at I. 11. a. Sheet 57.B	
JEUNE BOIS	15-10-18		Lieut. G.T. COLLINSON, proceeded to U.K. for transfer to R.A.F.	
—	21-10-18		Head Qrs, Nos 1, 2, & S.A.A. Sections proceeded via BETHENCOURT to camps located at J. 3. c. Sheet 57.B	
PREMELLE	23-10-18		2nd Lieuts I.T. JAMES and N. PEACOCK, posted from Base	
—	24-10-18		Head Qrs. Nos 1 & 2 Sections and S.A.A. Section, proceeded via VIESLEY & BRIASTRE to camps located at E. 13. a. Sheet 57.B	
SOLESMES	24-10-18		Captain C.I. SCOWCROFT, posted to 211th Bde R.F.A., and Captain R. HARTLEY posted from 211th Bde R.F.A.	

(CONTINUED to Sheet 2.)

SHEET 2. OCTOBER 1918. 42nd DIV. AMM. COLUMN

Volume XXII

WAR DIARY or INTELLIGENCE SUMMARY.

Army Form C. 2118.

(Erase heading not required.)

Place	Date	Hour	Summary of Events and Information	Remarks and references to Appendices
SOLESMES	26.10.18		2nd Lieuts. T.T. JAMES, and N. PEACOCK, posted to 210th Brigade R.F.A. Head Qrs. Nos 1, 2 and S.A.A. Sections proceeded on ROMERIES to combat at W.22.d. Sheet 51.A.	
	24.10.18		The undermentioned were the arrivals and departures during this month.	

ARRIVALS.

	OFF.	O.R.
Posted from Base (British)	2	149
do. (Indian)		
Posted from 211th Bde. R.F.A.	2	2
Rejoined from Hospital		3
Returned from leave to U.K.	5	94
Posted from 42nd T.M. Brigade	1	
Posted from 1/2nd East Lancs. T. Bmdt.	1	-

DEPARTURES.

	OFF.	O.Rs.
Proceeded to U.K. for Kooper R.A.F.	1	1
Posted to Base (Indian)		
Posted to 210th Bde. R.F.A.	4	85
Posted to 211th Bde. R.F.A.	3	43
Posted to R.A.H.Qrs		2
Admitted to Hospital	1	12.
Proceeded to U.K. on leave	4	43
Posted to 5th Division	1	-

H. Dermel — MAJOR R.F.A.
COMMANDING, 42nd DIV. AMM. COLUMN.

98 22

Confidential
War Diary
of

42nd Divisional Ammunition Column.

From 1st November, 1918. to 30th November, 1918.

Volume XXIII.

WAR DIARY or INTELLIGENCE SUMMARY

Army Form C. 2118.

42nd Div. Amm. Column

VOLUME XXIII

NOVEMBER 1918

Place	Date	Hour	Summary of Events and Information	Remarks and references to Appendices
ROUVROIS	1.11.18		Distribution of Unit:- Head Qrs. N°s 1, 2 & S.A.A. Sections at W.22.d. Sh.51 S.1.9	
"	1.11.18		2nd Lieut. R. GOLDSBROUGH posted from Base.	
"	6.11.18		Head Quarter, N°s 1, 2, & S.A.A. Sections moved via BEAUDIGNIES & LE QUESNOY to camp at M.22.c. Sheet 51	
PONT BISSON	7.11.18		Head Quarter, N°s 1 & 2 Sections moved to HERBIGNIES, M.30.a.m.2. Sheet 51	HMB
HERBIGNIES	12.11.18		Head Quarter, N°s 1 & 2 Sections moved to camps at V.30.b.2. O.33.d.6.2. and O.29.A.6.2 respectively	
LA GROISE	19.11.18		S.A.A. Section moved from PONT BISSON via FOREST-de-MORMAL to camp at O.34.B.6.6. Sheet 51.	
"	29.11.18		N°2 Section moved to camp at O.2h.a.2.2. Sheet 51.	
			The undermentioned were the arrivals and departures during the month	
			ARRIVALS.	
				O. O.R.
			Posted from Base (British)	0 39.
			do (Indian)	1 3.
			Posted from 211th Bde. R.F.A.	5
			Rejoined from leave to U.K.	2 40
			Rejoined from Hospital (British)	8
			DEPARTURES.	HMB
				O. O.R.
			Posted to 210th Bde. R.F.A.	0 154
			Posted to 211th Bde R.F.A.	107
			Posted to T.M. Bde	12
			Admitted to Hospital (British)	25
			Proceeded to U.K. on leave	1 28
			Admitted to Hospital (Indian)	15

H.W. Barnes
Major R.F.A.
Commanding, 42nd D.A.C.

WD 23

Confidential.

War Diary
of
42nd Divisional Amm. Column.

From 1-12-1918 to 31-12-1918.

Volume XXIV.

Army Form C. 2118.

WAR DIARY
or
INTELLIGENCE SUMMARY.

(Erase heading not required.)

42nd Div. Amm. Column.

VOLUME XXIV

DECEMBER 1918

Instructions regarding War Diaries and Intelligence Summaries are contained in F. S. Regs. Part II. and the Staff Manual respectively. Title pages will be prepared in manuscript.

Place	Date	Hour	Summary of Events and Information	Remarks and references to Appendices
LA COTTNE	1.12.18		Distribution of Unit :- Headquarters 0.33.a.6.5. No 1 Section 0.33.d.6.2. No 2 Section 0.34.a.2.2. S.A.A Section 0.34.b1.5. all Sheet 51	
LA COTTNE	14.12.18		HQrs. No 1, No 2 & S.A.A. Sections moved to MARPENT.	AHB
MARPENT	15.12.18		H.Qrs. No 1, No 2 & S.A.A. Sections moved to LOBBES, BELGIUM.	
LOBBES	18.12.18		H.Qrs. No 1, No 2 & S.A.A. Sections moved to CHATELINEAU, BELGIUM.	AHB
			The undermentioned were the arrivals & departures during the month	
			— ARRIVALS — — DEPARTURES —	
			Posted from Base (British) O.R. 97 Posted to 210 Bde R.F.A. O.R. 44	
			do do do (Indian) 8 do do 211 do do 40	
			do do 211 Brigade R.F.A. 1 do do 42nd T.M.B. 1	
			do do 1st Division 1 Admitted to Hospital (British) 16	
			Rejoined from Hospital 6 do do do (Indian) 10	
			do do do (British) 1 Proceeded to U.K. for	
			do do do (Indian) demobilization,	
			do do Leave to U.K. 24 Posted to Base 36	
			Proceeded to U.K. on leave 3 35	

H.H. Arnot
Major R.F.A.
Comdg 42nd D.A.C.

CONFIDENTIAL.

WAR DIARY
— OF —
42nd DIVISIONAL AMMUNITION COLUMN.

VOLUME XXV.

FROM:- 1st JANUARY 1919.
TO:- 31st JANUARY 1919.

Army Form C. 2118.

WAR DIARY
of
INTELLIGENCE SUMMARY.
(Erase heading not required.)

42nd Div. Amm. Column.

VOLUME XXV.

Place	Date	Hour	Summary of Events and Information	Remarks and references to Appendices
CHATELINEAU. BELGIUM.	1-1-19 to 31-1-19		Distribution of Unit:- Headquarters, Nos. 1, 2 and S.A.A. Sections :- CHATELINEAU, BELGIUM.	A/B
			The undermentioned were the Arrivals and Departures during the month:-	
			ARRIVALS.	
			O. O.R.	
			Posted from Base (British) 1 6	
			do. do. (Indian) 14	
			do. do. 5th D.A.C. 1	
			do. do. 211 Bde. R.F.A. 9	
			do. do. R.A.H.Q. 1	
			do. do. 42 T.M.Bde. 1	
			Rejoined from Hospital (British) 3	
			do. do. (Indian) 2	
			do. do. Leave to U.K. 2 9	
			DEPARTURES.	
			O. O.R.	A/B
			Posted to 210 Bde. R.F.A. 1	
			do. do. 211 Bde. 12	
			do. do. R.A.H.Q. 3	
			Admitted to Hospital (British) 11	
			do. (Indian) 8	
			Proceeded to U.K. for demobilization 108	
			do. do. Leave 2 32	
			Struck off Strength 1 1	

H.C. Brown
Major R.F.A.
Commanding 42nd D.A.C.

CONFIDENTIAL.

WAR DIARY

OF

42ND. Div. Amm. Column (Incld 42ND TMB).

VOLUME XXVI.

From. 1ST. FEBY 1919.   To. 28TH. FEBY 1919.

Army Form C. 2118.

WAR DIARY
or
INTELLIGENCE SUMMARY.
(Erase heading not required.)

42ND Div Amm Column (Including 42nd Div TMS).
VOLUME XXVI.

Place	Date	Hour	Summary of Events and Information	Remarks and references to Appendices
Chatelineau Belgium	1-2-19 to 28-2-19		Distribution of Unit:— Headquarters Nos 1 & 2 and S.A.A. Sections. Chatelineau. Belgium. The undermentioned were the Arrivals and Departures during the month. — ARRIVALS — O. ORs. Posted from Base (Indians) 4 42nd T.M.B. 49. Rejoined from Hospital (British) 5. — DEPARTURES — O. ORs. Admitted to Hospital (British) 1 21. " (Indian) 42. Left for Demobilization 4 58.	MB

H.W. Browne
Major R.F.A.
Comdg 42nd. D.A.C.

CONFIDENTIAL.

WAR DIARY

of

42ND. DIV. AMM. COLUMN & T.M.B.

From 1.3.1919. To 31st. 3. 1919.

VOLUME. XXVII.

Army Form C. 2118.

WAR DIARY 42ND DIV Amm COLUMN Including 42ND Div TMS.
or
INTELLIGENCE SUMMARY. VOLUME XXVII
(Erase heading not required.)

Place	Date	Hour	Summary of Events and Information	Remarks and references to Appendices
CHATELINEAU 1/3/19 BELGIUM 14/3/19			Distribution of Unit:	
			Headquarters Nos 1 + 2 and S.A.A. Section CHATELINEAU BELGIUM.	
	14.3.19.		63 ORs attached to 210th Bde for duty.	
			64 " " " 211th " " "	
			All Indian Personnel attached to 210th and 211th Bdes for duty.	
	14.3.19		Remainder move to MONTIGNY NEUVILLE, BELGIUM.	
	29.3.19.		35 ORs rejoined Unit from attachment to 210th Bde RFA	
			35 " " " " " 211th Bde "	
			The undermentioned were the arrivals & departures during the month.	

ARRIVALS
Rejoined from hospital (British)   0 OR.
" " " (Indian)   1
Posted from RA Hqrs. (British)   2.
" " 211th Bde   9
" " 42nd TMB   15.
   1

DEPARTURES
Admitted to Hospital (British)   0. OR.
" " " (Indian)   4.
Left for demobilization   5.
Posted to 210th Bde RFA.   3   9.
" " 211th "   -   33.
   4   30.

ANIMALS
	HORSES.	MULES.
To Base.		42
Sold.	40	279
= 210th + 211th Bdes RFA	38.	210

County 42nd TMB Major RFA
42nd DAC

www.ingramcontent.com/pod-product-compliance
Lightning Source LLC
Chambersburg PA
CBHW081240170426
43191CB00034B/1990